Conqueror of Counterfeit
LOVE

Conqueror of Counterfeit LOVE

Dr. Helen V. Robinson

CONQUEROR OF COUNTERFEIT LOVE
Copyright © 2017 Dr. Helen V. Robinson

All rights reserved.

No part of this book may be reproduced, distributed or transmitted in any form by any means, graphics, electronics, or mechanical, including photocopy, recording, taping, or by any information storage or retrieval system, without permission in writing from the publisher, except in the case of reprints in the context of reviews, quotes, or references.

Printed in the United States of America

ISBN: 978-0-692-93962-8

DEDICATION

To my husband, I love you.

To my children, grandchildren—Titus, Jasiyah, Aria, and Sidney—and those to come.

To family and friends who I love with the love of God.

PREFACE

The focus of this book is to provide a genuine insight on this four-letter word: Love. It aims to help people make better choices with relationships that may or may not lead to marriage covenants in the not-so-distant future.

This book have been in the works, on and off, for nine years. I deeply motivated to write these chapters by my desire to share true passion with a creditable and acceptable partner. The subject matter of love is very close to my heart, and I've always been fascinated with love and the act of loving.

We all need love and I am love.

TABLE OF CONTENTS

Introduction 1

CHAPTER ONE
The Camouflage of Love 3

CHAPTER TWO
Unequal Treatment 9

CHAPTER THREE
Love in the Middle 13

CHAPTER FOUR
A More Excellent Way to Love 19

CHAPTER FIVE
A Reversed Heart 23

CHAPTER SIX
The Art of Love-N-Me 27

CHAPTER SEVEN
A Love Relationship Undressed 33

CHAPTER EIGHT
Abiding Victoriously in Love 37

CHAPTER NINE
More than Conqueror 41

CHAPTER TEN
A New Beginning 45

My Prayer for You 51

About the Author 53

INTRODUCTION

Ladies and gentlemen, we are the apex of God's creation and we need love. Love is what created us, for God Himself is love (1 John 4:7-8). We breathe love constantly. It was love that blew the breath of life in us and we became living souls (Genesis 2:7). In other words, we are living souls of love, and the Bible further advises us to love one another. It is so easy to declare and proclaim that God loves us, and yet we fall so, so, far from loving one another and others like we were created to do.

Conqueror of Counterfeit Love is intended to stir up the spirit, shift your mindset, and lift the scales off the eyes to see love with an authentic view. To all readers, women and men, thank you in advance for your support by selecting this book. It is my prayers that you'll always remain in the state of love.

Chapter One

THE CAMOUFLAGE OF LOVE

You want unconditional love, one that sees no wrong and does no wrong. But instead, you accept love that deceives and hurts, pretends to be the real thing when it's only counterfeit. When love is masked or camouflaged, it blends with lies and causes your feelings and emotions to become distorted, leaving you numb.

Exposure is key to turning counterfeit love upside down and inside out. Simply remove the camouflage or expose it by being honest—tell the truth. The Bible tells us the truth will set you free: Once the deceit is exposed and dealt with, the healing process can begin.

With that being said, knowing the difference between what is real and what is not isn't so easy when it comes to love, because it is a rare commodity that everyone seeks and many do not take the time to examine; they just accept what's available at face value. Everything that looks good is not always good; after all, looks truly can be deceiving.

Words spoken are also important, but some words can be or become empty containers. It's wonderful when people are one with what they say, but any man or a woman can paint a beautiful picture for you with words; sometimes, we do it to peak interest in another person, but the picture created by words can only truly be seen when its carried out by actions.

When non-love is mistaken for love, it causes traffic jams within our minds and hearts, and if not corrected, it leaves our lives in ruins. If you deal with the counterfeit love long enough, you will become convinced that it is real thing. The kicker is, no matter how closely it resembles and feels real, it will still leave you unfulfilled and disappointed.

Counterfeit love will offer you a trip to an amusement park where you see pretty things and enjoy lots of games and rides. When you've been in a relationship for a while (ten years like I was), it is possible to become blinded to the camouflage and counterfeit. In addition, fear of confronting false love because you think you might not get it back makes it seem appropriate to make fake love appear authentic, even when you know it's not. This is selfish behavior.

Now, how can you get past this behavior and conqueror counterfeit love? First, you must understand what love is. One definition of love is: An intense feeling of deep affection that is moved into action for the greater good of the recipient. John 3:16 tells us that God so loved us (intense feeling of deep affection) that He gave us His only begotten Son (moved into action) so that whosoever believeth shall not perish but have everlasting life (for our greater good). This love is unconditional, authentic, and full of action, superseding lip service and empty promises.

Second, you must examine your own self. Be honest and open with your partner in expressing your feelings, and listening to when he or she expresses his or her feelings in return. Ask lots of questions and expect honest answers. Communicate effectively by making sure that what is stated is understood by the receiver.

Third, become familiar with the characteristics or behavior of an individual that could be camouflaging, pretending, faking, and playing with love. Here is a suggested list of characteristics in such an individual (and this list is in no way exhaustive):

- ☑ Comes to you when it's convenient because you're an option, not a priority
- ☑ Absent on important dates like birthdays and holidays
- ☑ Tells lies and makes excuses
- ☑ Makes promises but never fulfills them
- ☑ Doesn't spend much time or invest money in relationship

You probably can think of more characteristics that should be added. When you've conquered counterfeit love, you can feel safe from hurt, just as God's love makes you feel safe and saved with an expected end; only counterfeit love makes you feel unsafe and troubled.

Fourth, surrender your bad feelings and emotions of what someone did to you. In all respects, the offense was not only committed against you but also God, and the offender will answer for them (Matthew 25:45). You must take off the camouflage and let the light of love navigate you through this life's journey.

I came face to face with counterfeit love in the form of a man who didn't know how to love me like I deserved to be loved or like Christ's love. Instead, the love I was receiving was unhealthy and it put me in a web that made me go along to get along; I found myself always on the giving end and receiving little to nothing back. Who was fooling whom? Was it love or lust?

It's a hurtful thing to love somebody for so long, only to find out that, after all that time, it was all a game. Healing may be uncomfortable but you must stay in the process of releasing all the bad and hurt so God can fill you with His love again. Humble yourself and forgive the other person who is responsible for the pain, even though this may not be an easy thing for some to do. The love you deserve can only be found in Jesus.

We live in a world awash with love stories. However, most of them are nothing but lust and sex fantasy stories, just to name a few. Not only do these lies mess up our human relationships, but they also mess up our relationships with God. But we can be cured of all the sentimentalized and neurotic distortions of love that incapacitate us from truly loving others who also love us back, and move towards restoring ourselves in God, who loves us endlessly.

Chapter Two

UNEQUAL TREATMENT

What's in it for me? That's the question we often ask. But the Bible tell us, "Love your enemies, bless them that curse you, do good to them that hate you, and pray for them that despitefully use you and persecute you" (Matthew 5:44). Now, just because it's written doesn't mean it's not hard or awkward—it definitely is. This part of the journey was hard for me. As I started to learn and understand the proper way one must be treated (with kindness, respect, and love), it was time to put a demand on myself that I no longer tolerate and act as if I appreciate such mistreatment.

Some people seek out low self-esteem in others and exploit it—this may lead to severe abuse and mistreatment in such cases. Once it is recognized then separation is not an option, it is the antidote. Yes, according to Scripture I will love you and bless you and certainly pray and do good to those who hate and despitefully use and persecute me, but it will be from afar.

Are you being treated based on how you think of yourself? Think about that question. Are you accepting the treatment you are receiving because you see your image as somehow lesser or undeserving? Remember that you are made in God's image, and His image is best. You must conform to His image and not to that of the world. The standard and boundaries that you set must be aligned with the word of God. When you are exposed to unfair treatment, you must determine the best way for you to dismantle and resolve the affects that force you to see yourself in anything less than a divine light.

Now, unequal looks like this: Two moral, free agents that have different ideas and views on religion and life who can't come together and be on the same page about anything. When in a relationship, if you and your partner do not believe in the same principles or are unable to walk in agreement, it can lead to disturbances and awkward adjustments to the life balance. Being on one accord promotes and facilitates peace, stability, equality, and harmony in your relationship. I am not saying that disagreements will not rise—it's just that, on an equal scale, the treatment is fair and the debate and conversation is enriching for both parties.

Lies and deception by either party will cause unequal or unfair treatment. Keeping one in the dark is not wise, for what is done in the dark, will come to the light. Do unto other as you would like done to you is a classic rule of thumb, (Matthew 7:12)—if you are treating others with love and respect, it is natural for you to desire to be treated the same. Even when you may not receive the same love in return, do not allow that other person to rob you of the innate love and kindness you have inside. That person who is worthy of receiving what you offer and who will reciprocate that honor is not far away.

So, what should you do when you are exposed to unfair treatment? Confront it or treat it? I opt to treat it by making wrong right again and exposing wrong through light. Stop settling for what you think you want or what presents itself to want you. Take the time to pray and remember that love does not hurt, nor is it self-seeking—love is God and God is love (Corinthians 13). God did not treat you or me the way we deserve as sinners, because Jesus took that treatment for us on the cross at Calvary. We were loved even when we were in a pool of sin, on our way to hell. He made a way to redeem us back to Him and that was through His Son, Jesus. Can we demonstrate this love toward those who mistreat us?

I've endured unequal treatment for a long time, not on one occasion but several times. I then asked the question: Why endure such pain to show another person unconditional love? I then realized that this was the exact kind of love that was once shown toward me by Christ: Jesus went through much pain even unto death to demonstrate His love for me. Of course, this didn't justify the treatment I was receiving, but it made me see that I was capable of such loving—the love of God. I made a choice to not get even and forgive instead, keeping my love of God intact.

Anger sometime sets in and makes everything else in the relationship unbearable and unbalanced. The anger must be restrained to the point that it does not infest the relationship and put it on the road of destruction. Satan comes to kill, steal, and destroy, and any treatment that is not pure, just, or right is of the enemy. Remember that the enemy wanted to be God, which means he wants to be treated like God—he wants you to put him first in your life. As the story goes, what Satan attempted to do cost him his position in heaven. Will you let your desire to unleash anger cost you your position of being in a good and healthy relationship with God?

The power of thinking before acting is key to treat yourself and others with respect and honesty. Forgiveness is another key that will allow you to move forward and push past the undeserved mistreatment of counterfeit love.

Chapter Three

LOVE IN THE MIDDLE

Yes, it is exciting when you first meet your lover and you start sharing your time together, getting to know more about each other. Anything in the beginning is exciting, often times because it is uncertain, just like starting a new job or getting a new car. It's a blooming period of happiness, a fun time. After all, we all want and deserve the best, and that includes loving and stable relationships.

But love in the middle, or "in the meantime love," is what is expressed and demonstrated between excitement and commitment, when the highs and peaks of the relationship seem to have sunk into the valley. It sometimes drifts downwards instead of upward towards commitment; sometimes it goes into a spinning cycle and will appear as if the person is stuck. How did I get here? What happened? Is it over? Many questions come to mind when we reach this point in the relationship. Can I love him or her while (in the meantime) he or she is lying and cheating and doing all sorts of other things? Can I still love him or her (in the meantime) when I know they can't be trusted?

It can be an uncomfortable place to be, but so very necessary to strengthen any relationship, especially when it requires endurance and tries and tests our faith and trust. The process is much more bearable when you know who you are and have established boundaries and standards for that relationship. A woman or man cannot define you, but love *can* define you. 1 Corinthians 13:4-8 gives a very descriptive picture of love:

> "Love endures long and is patient and kind; love never is envious nor boils over with jealousy, is not boastful or vainglorious, does not display itself haughtily.
>
> It is not conceited (arrogant and inflated with pride); it is not rude (unmannerly) and does not act unbecomingly. Love (God's love in us) does not insist on its own rights or its own way, for it is not self-seeking; it is not touchy or fretful or resentful; it takes no account of the evil done to it [it pays no attention to a suffered wrong].
>
> It does not rejoice at injustice and unrighteousness, but rejoices when right and truth prevail.
>
> Love bears up under anything and everything that comes is ever ready to believe the best of every person, its hopes are fadeless under all circumstances, and it endures everything [without weakening].

Love never fails [never fades out or becomes obsolete or comes to an end]. As for prophecy (the gift of interpreting the divine will and purpose), it will be fulfilled and pass away; as for tongues, they will be destroyed and cease; as for knowledge, it will pass away [it will lose its value and be superseded by truth]".

These words are something to hold onto when you're in the middle of love. I was in the middle and some of you may be in the middle right now or even heading straight there, but this love will see you through as it has seen me through. I am better from this experience.

You see, I can't go on without love. Love is my essence of living and state of being, and to be effective and useful for my divine purpose on earth, I must love. It's not what I do, but who I am and becoming. But loving unconditionally isn't easy: As a matter of fact, I only felt that kind of love existed and knew it was real when I gave my life to God and later, much later, I was assured that He loved me and that I am love. From that point on, I was striving to express unconditional love to those who came across my path, because loving unconditionally is an unselfish act and it's all God. I can't love except through the love of God that is within me, so that mankind may have the advantage of God's love that is shared abroad in my heart.

Love in the middle transcends our reasoning and is a test of the continuous act of kindness and caring we can have towards one another. It propels you to be consistent in the relationship, not being up and down, based on what he or she is doing or not doing; it allows the seed of unconditional love to grow and sprout in our hearts towards those who may appear unlovable. Look at Jesus who hung in the middle between man and God: He is love in the middle for all of us. He died for you, not because you asked him to, but because it was in His divine purpose to bring you back or keep you connected to love. He didn't do anything, nor did he deserve to go the distance of death for our sin, but love in the middle was necessary to reconcile us back to love creator. It was love that stood in the gap for you and I, that washed and paid the penalty for our sins through bloodshed by Jesus, that reconnected us back to our creator God—what a love was demonstrated from the Cross!

As I personally examined the Cross, I saw that forgiveness was critical to moving forward. Love in the middle has tested and tried you, your emotions, your will, and your desires, and yet, you're still here. Well, love in the middle was not to break you but to strengthen your walk in love and build your love character in all you do. So, now, you must forgive and let go. Stop looking back to what was; that's not the direction you are going in anymore. Forgiveness only strengthens and prepares you to love again. It will take you dying to self and your selfish attitude to release such power of forgiveness to take the next step forward.

Now, with that being said, some of you may ask: Is love in the middle time to throw in the towel? Many of you reading this would say yes, depending on where you are in the relationship. Well, it is a personal choice and no one can do anything but make suggestions as to what you may want to consider doing. I suggest that you pray and embrace the time to conduct an introspection of self to determine if you yourself contributed to the faults in your relationship. Then, examine your relationship and desires for what they really are. You may want commitment in hopes that the excitement will continue or never end. But let's get real: Excitement has its purpose, and sometimes (even most times), you go through a phase called contentment. The problem is you may have confused contentment with commitment.

Love in the middle was indeed a cycle for me: I went through the pre-wash and then a soaking period…just soaking, waiting for the wash to begin. Did I need someone to push the wash button to get it going? No, not really—I should've just waited on the Lord. Too often, we want to skip a cycle to get to the finish but it is critical to go through the process; for instance, don't just get in bed with another person or buy him or her things because you think that will keep him or her all to yourself—news flash: It will not!

In the soaking phase, I checked areas in my life that I had *not* allowed God to come in through His Word to wash and cleanse me of my inability to forgive, which had turned my heart bitter. My bad attitude and poor conduct caused me to stray from the will of God for my life. It was then I realized that I didn't mind the soaking phrase. I needed and continue to need Jesus, who is my cleansing agent, for only He can wash away my stains from my sick soul and cause me to gain eternal life. He will do the same for you. At the end of my middle of love, all I wanted to do was forgive and say thanks to my un-loving lover for giving me the opportunity to love more unconditionally.

Love in the middle is real, people. Life is not all about you, but about Jesus…well, love in the middle will allow you to love like it is not about you and it is all about Jesus! Love in the middle does not have eyes that see like the world sees (that's merely sight), but has vision that only sees the best and good God created in you as well as in others.

We are more than conquerors. I am an overcomer of counterfeit love and I'm not deceived any longer by the sample the world displays, for it is a counterfeit.

Chapter Four

A MORE EXCELLENT WAY TO LOVE

Doing things in order is the most perfect way to live and efficiently perform activities in this universe. When thinking back as to how God took the time to organize the world even before He performed His apex creation (that's you and me), He made sure things were in its proper place. Then He put us in it, not put it in us: "You're in the world but not of it" (John 17:16).

This chapter is about organizing yourself and performing the way you were created. We must be and do everything in the order we were created to perform. I believe our shortcoming comes from failing to believe without seeing. The human organism is so used to only believing what we see that we feel challenged when facing the Spirit of God. The more excellent way to do things is to do in love and per God's instructions through His Words, which tells us that we can do anything and everything, but without love, we profit nothing (1 Corinthians 13: 3). Our love for God is the best way to love others. This type of action speaks volume.

To express love only to who or what loves you is your reward, and it has been said repeatedly that it's better to give than to receive. However, issues come into play when the motive for giving is for self-gain and not to reflect the love of God. At the same time, to love an individual who does not love you back because he or she may not know how to do so is like storing treasure and never finding it again.

So what's this all about? What amount do we give and what amount should we receive? Unconditional love is immeasurable: The density given equates to the density of what you have already received. In other words, sharing unconditional love based on the love you received sets the parameter as to how much you'll give, to whom, and how long you will give.

If we look to His Word, we see that Jesus put in all his work so that we could carry on in His work. There is a balance, but it all begins with you, as it did for Jesus. Your foundation must be love and everything done or said should stem from that solid foundation. Such a strong base that inspires love will attract others to be empowered by love. From that standpoint, avoid simply looking at what the other person can do for you. When you can stop looking how love is *performed*, you may find that you and the other person share more in common than you thought.

The sum of a more excellent way is love. Love that does not keep account of what was done or not done, what was given or received, what was said or not said. Love does not do unto you as you did unto me. Your trust and confidence in God will give you the assurance that His will be done and, as He is glorified, you will be satisfied beyond comparison.

Chapter Five

A REVERSED HEART

My heart has been broken before and I thought I would not be able to go on. Couldn't eat or sleep, couldn't function because my life was in pieces. Little did I know that, one day, I would be okay; as a matter of fact, I am better than okay: I'm well. And so are you. Thank You, Jesus.

The bitterness I had allowed to fester in my heart caused me to be less than nice towards others, especial the opposite sex. I blamed and resented the person who caused this injury that no one could see, but only I could feel, which made me angry and self-involved. It was as if my heart was turned upside down and the love I once knew and shared had turned into stone. My heart was captured by the lies, deception, and empty promises, which webbed my love and numbed my feelings. Even when I tried to free myself and cut loose one of these webs, there came another lie, another empty promise, that would spin me back into the web.

It's amazing to me that the heart connects to everything. When the heart is hurt or seems upside down, confusion settles quickly. Even when you know what's going on, there remains an ache in the heart that just won't go away. In this situation, love is not flowing properly and the heart needs to be restored back to its original health before you can move on.; and let me tell you, when the heart is not right, nothing else can go well. People often told me to "just go with your heart." I don't think they truly understand this phrase: When your heart has been broken by another's actions or lack of actions, it is in no place to speak for you: "Out of the abundance of the heart the mouth speaks" (Matthew12:34). Unconditional love is the right position the heart should be in, not love based on conditions placed upon you by another person—his or her heart is also reversed and the motives are not valid but selfish.

Misdirection and lack of focus will cause your heart to be in the wrong place. There is a way that seems right to man, but in actuality, it leads to destruction (Proverbs 14:12). When your heart is yielded to the way *you* plan, then one can expect to experience obstacles and even failures while on that journey. When we handle issues improperly and make decisions outside the wisdom and knowledge of God's Word, we turn our hearts hard and callous. By failing to acknowledge Him who keeps us from leaning on our own understanding, we reverse our hearts away from the ways of God.

As I examined myself daily to ascertain what I had allowed to enter my heart, I got rid of destructive emotions such as hatred, anger, bitterness, resentment, and pride right away. Why? Because, I was not being a blessing to others, and more importantly, I was stopping my own fruitful growth to be a blessing to myself. Make sure to check your heart's direction every day; most of us have no problem checking ourselves out physically, the exterior, to see if everything is in place, but very few take the time to check out the heart to see what's in it.

Forsake yourself and turn back; forsake yourself to your first love: God (Revelation 2:4). He was my first love, and all I know about the spirit of love has been revealed from Him by His Spirit. It took me a long time to love again but, today, I am free and my reversed heart that was once bitter and angry is no longer. The love of God has turned my heart and me around, saved my soul, and set me free from the web of counterfeit love. I'm a conqueror of counterfeit love.

Chapter Six

THE ART OF LOVE-N-ME

Discovering who I am was the beginning of the art of loving me: A fashioned woman with beauty and strength from God to be a sufficient partner to the created man. I often asked myself many times: What is love? What does it feel like? What does it look like? How does one love? I had lots of questions about love that no one knew the answers for, which led me on this journey of seeking God to understand love for myself—what it did was lead me into a closer relationship with God who taught me to start loving how He fashioned me to love.

So, what is love? Biblically, love is God and God is love (1 John 4:8). I didn't discover this until many years later. In the beginning, love to me was a feeling wrapped up with emotions and sweet words. But this is another side of counterfeit love. In God's truth, love is infallible. Love is commitment. Love is the glue that holds everything together.

Love is who you are, as well as what you do, think, and give. Why is it that people are always looking for you to do something, think a certain way, and give of yourself all because you used this four-letter word? It could be because, when people do not love themselves, they expect others—or you—to love them more. Compromising situations present themselves to us all the time and we often respond to it based on *our* understanding of love or on the love we receive from the other person.

Ladies and gentlemen, stop making others your priority when they intentionally and purposely choose to make you their option. Start learning to love you for you so you can love others and others know how to love you! Follow these steps to loving yourself the way God designed you to love:

- ☑ Discover who you are: Examine your life and the relationships you have had. You will most likely discover why you love the way you do. You may gain a greater understanding of your make-up (attributes that contribute to your actions) and you will accept who you are. Then, you will have a greater expectation of what is acceptable to give and receive from others, especially your significant other.

- ☑ Define the love you are: As you discover who you are and start loving yourself, you will experience a definitive love that will supersede all your prior knowledge of love. In this step, you should embrace your whole self—start loving every part of you. Each part of you serves love to the whole of you, so love all parts of you (feet, hands, legs, etc.). No longer take yourself for granted but love yourself unconditionally.

☑ Demonstrate the love are: Now that you have discovered yourself and have defined love, demonstrate step one and two collectively: Show the art of love-n-me to others so they can have the advantage of God's love in you being shown unto to them. Remember the words "Love your neighbor as you love yourself" (Mark 12:31) and "Love others as Jesus has loved you" (John 15:12).

I had to learn to not allow someone to treat me (which they called "loving" me), in such a way that was not acceptable and not in accordance with how God desires me to be loved. It was a time when I wanted love so desperately, I found myself loving what "loved" me, only to ascertain later it wasn't love at all: It was lust and I was being pinned into a web of deception. Better yet, I was deceiving myself. I said I wanted out, but all my actions showed I wanted in more than I wanted to be free from that counterfeit love. Have you found yourself wanting to be out of a relationship of counterfeit love, but the strong pull of your desire causes you to stay in that mess?

Disappointment after disappointment, lie after lie, hurt and more hurt, nights of crying, days of no returned calls or texts…that was it. I had had enough. I wanted to be free from it all. I began by looking in the mirror and saying to the image that the natural eyes could see, "You deserve better, more, and greater." When I finally said this out loud, tears welled my eyes and I fell to my knees and cried out to God, "Help me to love like You and let me start loving Your fashioned woman so I can love others in-kind."

Again, the art of loving you is generated from how you see yourself, or rather, how God sees you. When you see what you see (sight), we only see the physical, but when we look at what is seen in the image and likeness of God, sight converts into vision. Spend time with God, get closer to Him through His Word, meditate on what you study, and listen to what God says while you commune with Him in private. Give praise and worship Him for taking care of and protecting you from the hands of the enemy, especially during times you think you are "loved," but are actually being mistreated.

Now, loving you is more than telling someone, "I am doing me now." Phrases like this only open the door for the enemy to war in your mind. This kind of speaking creates selfishness and bitterness to a greater degree than what already exists in the heart. Be encouraged and love yourself more because you know you are valuable to God and He does love you more than you can fathom.

Loving myself feels like a gentle breeze against my face and through my hair, and the comfort of holding hands. It feels like I am standing in the cool shade of a tree on a hot summer day, sharing one dessert with two spoons or a soda with one straw and purposely taking less so the other can enjoy more. It feels like being tucked safe and secure in my Father's arms because I'm the apple of His eye and He is carefully watching over me (Zechariah 2:8).

Only when you get this kind of understanding of love, will you truly know *how* to love. We must love through the spirit of love from God, which is unconditional love. It will pay off, to be humble and stay in a state of forgiveness; ultimately, your ability to love yourself and others unconditionally will act as a protective shield against the arrows of conditional love, which only says "If you love me, you will do this or that." You will need this most when you must love those you may deem unlovable and undeserving of your love.

The art of love-n-me is work, but it's a good work. You must pray daily, asking the Spirit of God to show and teach you more about His love, and how to love yourself and others in ways that reflect how He loves you. You are all my brothers and my sisters and I will demonstrate love towards all, especially the people of God. Amen.

Chapter Seven

A LOVE RELATIONSHIP UNDRESSED

Have you ever given thought to the differences between naked love and clothed love?

Before I begin, it's imperative that we truly understand what a relationship is. A relationship consists of two or more individuals making an agreement to be in partnership. The key element here is agreement. And did you know that agreement is a Biblical principle (Amos 3:3)? I realized that God created mankind to be in a relationship with Him as well as with one another.

A love relationship undressed is what God created when He made man and woman before the fall to sin. Love undressed is being transparent like clear water, nothing hidden, everything exposed, and most of all, being bare with honesty. When I first began thinking about this, I was in awe to discover how little I really knew about love. How can one conqueror something without understanding? To gain better comprehension, I studied His word and deeply considered what I Corinthians 13:4-8 (noted in Chapter Thirteen) had to say about love. This passage provided me with a clear picture of what love undressed should be and look like.

So, let me paint this picture of undressed love for you: My first stoke of paint from the brush reflects that I am not a jealous person; I have no intense desire to advance at the advantage of another, for I do not resent the success of my fellow brother and sisters in Christ. I will choose the color of paint, and it will not be green with envy and jealousy.

The second stroke of paint reveals that I am not selfish or boastful, and do not require adoration or acknowledgement from others; I do not toot my own horn and I do not have to explain my self-worth to anyone.

The third stroke of paint represents how I am not conceited and do not think I am better than anyone else; I am no better than you, and you are no better than me.

The fourth stroke from the brush says I do not fail to show respect and honor to others, especially to myself. I never disrespect myself, and no one deserves to do so to him or herself.

The fifth stroke is a bleeding line that says that I will not refuse to forgive someone who has wronged me. I will not keep records of all that has been done to me; instead, I will choose to let go. This does not come easily, but you can do it: Try forgiving someone today.

The sixth stroke comes down the middle and says that I can absorb everything with compassion, even the difficulties that I endure and others endure.

The seventh stroke illustrates that I have hope for all things and believe in all things; I possess an unshakable confidence in God and all His promises. Amen.

The eighth brush stroke boldly reflects a victorious new beginning despite every hardship and persecution that comes to me.

Finally, the ninth stroke is a big, enclosed, circular stroke that encompasses all the strokes, signifying that love never ends and that I will never let love become defunct or invalid in my life. I am this person and so are you. You are also this portrait of undressed love.

We all can conqueror counterfeit love. True love undressed is beautiful, stands alone, and is complete and everlasting. Keep this portrait in mind when you consider loving someone. Will you love undressed or remain fully clothed by outside influences, ways of man, and lies. Before any relationship, the first relationship you must establish is one with God. Having this undressed love relationship with God will be the measure of all other relationships formed in your life. Your relationships with others will not be any better than your relationship with God. Love undressed means God first!

Chapter Eight

ABIDING VICTORIOUSLY IN LOVE

We are victorious! If you are unable to declare this statement now, I pray that, by the time you reach the end of this book, you will be able to shout, "I am victorious!"

Everyone likes being a winner. There is a winner inside of you and one in inside of me, and yes, it's the same winner. We cannot win without the Holy Spirit. I'm talking about being spiritually victorious in love. If this is not so, then what evidence in your life will justify that you are victorious when it comes to love? If we were all victorious in love then maybe the nation's divorce rate might be lower.

Many believe that they are successful at love until some unfavorable circumstance or situation arises. Many of you may have experienced temporary defeat in loving others. I was once guilty of this but now I learned how to just forgive and think of how God has loved me and still loves me in all my mess. So, despite what I would rather do, I did and still do what the Word of God says, "Love others as I have loved you" (John 13:34).

Being victorious in love does not mean that you will not have any issues or concerns, because you will. It means that you will be able to handle those problems properly in a loving manner, to the point that no further pain is experienced by either party. Just think for a moment of all the issues you experienced in your last relationship or maybe experiencing now in your current relationship. How did you handle them then and how are you going to handle them now? Some of you may have handled issues the way I used to: I'd think and act accordingly to "What you did to me, I will do to you," or just cut people from my life. But praise the Lord, that was then and this is now. I no longer hold on to anger. I have a better understanding now of what love is and how love behaves.

As you ponder the concerns you currently have or have had in the past, would you consider handling them in love so no further pain and hurt is experienced? We talk the talk but we can't or we choose not to walk the walk. After all, why should you be the one to say I'm sorry when you feel you haven't done anything? The truth is, recognizing and apologizing for your wrongs shows 1) your level of maturity, 2) your respect for Jesus' example of forgiveness, 3) your love of God forwarded to another, and 4) your role as a peacemaker. There are plenty of other reasons for why you should initiate healing by saying, "I'm sorry." If you can think of more reasons *not* to apologize, that's okay too. I hope from reading this book that there will be a change and shift in your thinking, as writing this book did for my mindset.

When you and I abide by love, we can live victoriously with ourselves and others. Abide means to conform, to act in accordance with and obey. Today is a new day, and you and I get a new start. I choose to abide victoriously by love and become the example that others would want to follow. Join me in this walk because the world needs people who love unconditionally.

Chapter Nine

MORE THAN CONQUEROR

You thought you wouldn't get through counterfeit love, but you did. Your clock has been reset and you are on another course, a fresh start. To be more than a conqueror is to not only overcome the enemy but also to find liberation in oneself. It is to be free. Free from the hurt and pain of disappointment after disappointments betrayal after betrayal, the lies told. But most importantly, to be more than a conqueror is to be free to forgive.

You can now take your stand. No longer will you sit back and accept what is dished out to you, especially when it is less than you deserve. If you know you deserve to be treated like a queen, then do not accept the treatment of a sex slave or doormat. If you know you deserve to be treated like a king, then do not accept the treatment of an errand boy. No longer will you be in a roller coaster relationship. The love you have for yourself will command you to be set apart from the foolishness and manipulations of the enemy.

Moving on to higher grounds now, your footing is secured and sure; whatever comes, you are strong enough to withstand against the odds, for greater is He that is within you than he that is in the world. Test and trials are sure to come but you are more than a conqueror and that means you can conqueror all, for Jesus declared that we are more.

Before writing this book, I was a mess and an emotional wreck, and yet I tried to love someone that was not interested in the love I desired to show and give. I did this for many years—people told me I was a fool, but I didn't feel like one. Doing foolish things, I get, but being a fool for love…I did not get it. Later, I understood what those folks were saying.

Lies can never be or become the truth. In coming into my more-than-a-conqueror state, I had to deal with all the lies that were told to me; sometimes, I knew he was telling lies and yet I chose to accept them as truths instead of dealing with the falsehood, all just to keep that man. I had to shake that thing off of me, so I fasted and prayed for forty days for my breakthrough, which carried me to a breakout that delivered me from what would have destroyed me to absolute ruins.

God has a plan for all of us. I took my plans and lay them down for the joy of the Lord. It was then I realized that my plans weren't plans at all but just some ideas that God did not buy in on. My mother once told me, "If you want to make God laugh, tell Him your plan." The Creator who holds the blueprint to my life—really, what can I tell Him? I can tell

Him, "Lord have your way with me." Are you willing to surrender your will to do His will? This is part of the process of becoming more than a conqueror, so you can be of assistance to others.

It's time for you to put yourself in God's plan. Just try Him—I'm sure once you get used to being in His plan, you will be glad you did. I am not where I once was and I no longer desire or want the things or that man who I once thought I couldn't go on without. The devil is a liar and, for a good ten years, he had me lying to myself. But God, opened my eyes and exposed all the darkness that was working to blacken my soul and consume my flesh, rendering me useless to God's plan and purpose for my life. That's what happens when you encounter light: It gives you a reflector view that makes you cry out to Jesus for help.

God protected me and got me through many things from bad relationships to disease. The soul ties I had to my partner in counterfeit love were too strong for me to break in my weakness but it was weightless to my omnipotent God. Trust God with all your giants. He slays and cuts them down right in their tracks. He is my Conqueror who conquerors all my enemies, and He will do the same for you.

If you are attached to something and you feel like you can't go on without it, then it has already captured you. So, reverse it! God made it possible for you and I to be free. Why enslave yourself for one more second? Don't commit the crime I did: I enslaved myself to one man for ten years, knowing that I had liberty to walk but still chose not to. But Jesus made me realize the emancipation that took place on the Cross through His shedding of blood. I am free!

If you'll go to the Master and get your marching orders from His Holy Spirit, you too will have the abilities to be more than a conqueror.

Chapter Ten

A NEW BEGINNING

As I reflect over my life and begin to write the closing chapter of this book, tears well up. I think of how good God has been to me over the years, especially in the last year, when He snatched me out of the grip of the enemy. Jesus came and got me out of Hell and reminded me of the keys *(binding and loosing)* He already gave me. Now, I am embracing my new beginning.

Ten years ago, I walked into a tunnel of darkness that I thought was love. I was captivated by the oohs and awes, but really, I was in captivity. I was there for a very long time, bound and shackled to counterfeit love. But God! God saw me in a state that was not His will for my life and I realized that I was more than what I had allowed a man to define me as.

Forty days I prayed and fasted, and I began to seek the presence of God for answers, direction, and instructions. I felt as if I was webbed into a wheel that was securely sealed and glued by all the lies, empty promises, and hot-air words that all convinced me that there was no possible way of escape. I needed Jesus, who is more powerful than those webs of lies, and have liberty, for which He died. God gave me the answers I needed.

When you have full confidence that you heard the voice of God, you are prepared to take appropriate action towards the instructions or direction spoken. Around the thirty-seventh day of the forty-day prayer, I heard God say, "He is not the one as he is now." At first, I was not sure if that was what I heard, for it wasn't what I was hoping to hear. But again, I heard, "He is not the one." I did not want to play dumb with God—I knew exactly who God was referring to. I cried and then I said, "Lord, you are the God of my life and you know what is best for me."

On the fortieth day, I shared with the other eight women of the Second Chance Outreach Ministry who were doing the prayer challenge with me about what I had heard God say about the man who I was hoping would be my spouse. They rejoiced and encouraged me. They told me, "God loves you so much that He snatched you from the grips of the enemy who had a plan to rob you of your peace and destroy your purpose to keep you from reaching your destiny."

God loves us so much that He will interrupt the enemy's designs to trick, trap, and destroy us from doing His will. I believe that because He did it for me, and I am so thankful. Can you think of one thing He did just for you that you can thank Him for? You can probably think of a few. Amen.

My God instantly put an end to what would have impeded my divine purpose. He showed me through my prayer and meditation of His Word that, as His child, I deserve better and my greater was coming. Thus, I turned, repented, and moved forward toward a new beginning, I was set free from the webs that had me bound and I thought to myself, it will just be me and God from now on. But God had another plan for me. He has a Master Plan.

It started back in 2008. This certain guy came to the church I was attending, and upon seeing me for the second time at the church's Family and Friend Day, he said to me, "I don't know why but God got you on my heart. I think you're supposed to be my wife." I said, "Boy, please," and kept on walking.

Many years passed, but he and I always remained friendly towards one another. I had started a ministry for domestic violence called Be W.H.O.L.E. (Women Healed and Overcoming through Love and Empowerment), and during the second year, he came aboard to help me with this ministry. He told me that he was on an assignment from God to aid me with, and indeed he did. When God sends the help, they really help: He cooked, handled the media, preached at ministry events, ran errands, and did everything I needed done and more. God was glorified and I was satisfied. Amen. God placed him there. Looking back over the times when he was there for me as a friend, I smile and say, "Yes, God had truly and sovereignly planted him in my life." Little did I know that he would become more to me than someone in the ministry.

Fast forward many years later, eight to be exact, God placed us back into each other's paths yet again. This time, I accepted the will of God for me to help him with the ministry God placed in him; and that's when God revealed to me that this man is a soulmate. God said, "He was always there, but you could not see, nor were you ready to receive him. But now, daughter, you are ready. Your greater is attached to this manservant. Put your trust in Me."

We must learn how to wait on God. It took me awhile to get that, and it is my prayer that it does not take as long for you. Once God helped me to let go, and completely let go, that's when He delivered the best for my spirit in this suit of flesh. The past is the past and that is where it belongs. As I venture on this new journey as a wife, I'm willing with the help of God to embrace new things. My new beginning will start with being married again to a man God chose for me. When many were unsure (even me), he remained the one. God knew. Many have asked us both at different times, "Are you sure?" I'm certain he says, "Yes!" I too say, "This is the will of God." Some are still doubtful, but they will rejoice with and for us anyways. Never think you know more than God or that you know what is best for you. I assure you, you don't.

In the near future, this man and I will be married in the presence of God, and a few of our love ones and friends to witness what the Lord has done for us. Our marriage is our ministry and, like anything else, it's work. Starting over again under the divine purview of the Holy Spirit, we shall walk in agreement and be obedient to the words and ways of the Almighty God. This union is not about us separately, but about God bringing the two into one for His will and purpose—our reward is that we get to share His love with each other and live rewarding lives.

Let me repeat again: Our lives are not our own, we do not belong to ourselves, and we cannot do what we think we want to do always and forever. God has a set time to bring our small thinking to a halt, but it will be when He is ready. Just the thought of God taking the rest of my life and merging it with the life of another is so loving and special. It shows that He loves me so much that He wants another human being to partake in His love that is shed in my heart. God is Love and Love is God—no one can fathom this kind of love. I'll walk through the rest of my life with my God-given husband, and I'll continue to love on God through him, for the word of God said in 1 John 4:20, "If a man say, I love God, and hateth his brother, he is a liar: for he that loveth not his brother whom he hath seen, how can he love God whom he hath not seen?"

"I love you." It's so easy to say, but to do is where so many of us trip up. To conqueror counterfeit love, you must be able to love the brothers and sisters you can see. This love is unconditional: It does not keep score, it does not get even, it does not make itself a priority or put itself first and make the other person an option, it does not seek to be served, it is not always on the receiving end. The time has come for us to get it right. If we work at it and trust in God, we can get this love business right.

If you are willing to be about your Father's business, well, His business is love. My new husband and I will love Him and each other and all those He will place in our path. To do otherwise will cost us a portion of our (money, sleep, job, health, etc.) without a substantial return.

Make your investment in love count and do it God's way. I'm finally living in my divine purpose of love and happiness for the rest of life. I thank God and I thank you for the time you took to read this book.

May God bless and love you.

MY PRAYER FOR YOU

Heavenly Father,

I acknowledge You as God and Father. I come to You in the name of Jesus who gave me access to Your throne; because of Your love for me, You gave Your only begotten son who bridges the gap between You and me. I pray to You, Lord, that the individual who reads this book will be filled in their hearts with Your unconditional love, which they can now receive and give. Lord God, I ask You to seed their hearts with love and make that love seed to grow so that they may forgive the hurt, lies, disappointment, cheating, deception, and manipulation that counterfeit love has caused.

I pray seeking prayer, Lord God, that they seek You first and seek to do and be righteous toward others. Lord, may they seek You and find You as the lover of their souls, lifter of their heads, their peace that surpasses all understanding and their ways, even when they believe there is no way. May they seek You, Lord God, to teach them and lead them in the path of what is right as they acknowledge You.

I pray, Lord God, as this individual comes to You knocking, open Your doors for them to walk through. Lord God, remove the hinges of the door, for You said that You will open doors that no man can close and You will close doors that no man can open. Father, in the name of Jesus, let situations be knocked out, circumstances be knocked over, trials and tribulations put down in the life of this individual so Your will and purpose be done in their life. Father, they are more than conquerors in Christ Jesus and let no weapon be formed against them prosper, Let Your unconditional love abide in them.

In Jesus' name. Amen.

ABOUT THE AUTHOR

Elder Helen Robinson is Director of Be W.H.O.L.E. (*Women Healed and Overcoming through Love and Empowerment*) Ministries located in Fort Washington, Maryland. Gifted with a strong teacher's calling, she has ministered throughout the United States and overseas missions in Central America. She is a sought-after conference speaker, and enjoys teaching, coaching, advising, and collaborating with others in the areas of relationships and life. She resides with her family in Maryland.

www.ingramcontent.com/pod-product-compliance
Lightning Source LLC
Chambersburg PA
CBHW072110290426
44110CB00014B/1885